To the Reader . . .

"World Cities" focuses on cities as a way to learn about the major civilizations of the world. Each civilization has at its roots the life of one or more cities. Learning about life in the great cities is essential to understanding the past and present of the world and its people.

People live in cities for many reasons. For one thing, they value what cities can offer them culturally. Culture thrives in all cities. It is expressed in visual arts, music, and ethnic celebrations. In fact, a city's greatness is often measured by the richness of culture that it offers those who live there.

Many people choose to live in cities for economic reasons. Cities offer a variety of jobs and other economic opportunities. Many city dwellers have found prosperity through trade. Nearly all the world's great cities were founded on trade—the voluntary exchange of goods and services between people. The great cities remain major economic centers.

City living can, of course, have its disadvantages. Despite these disadvantages, cities continue to thrive. By reading about the people, culture, geography, and economy of various metropolitan centers, you will understand why. You will also understand why the world is becoming more and more urban. Finally, you will learn what it is that makes each world city unique.

Mark Schug, Consulting Editor
Co-author of *Teaching Social Studies in the
Elementary School* and *Community Study*

CONSULTING EDITOR

Mark C. Schug
Professor of Curriculum and Instruction
University of Wisconsin-Milwaukee

EDITORIAL

Amy Bauman, Project Editor
Barbara J. Behm
Judith Smart, Editor-in-Chief

ART/PRODUCTION

Suzanne Beck, Art Director
Carole Kramer, Designer
Thom Pharmakis, Photo Researcher
Eileen Rickey, Typesetter
Andrew Rupniewski, Production Manager

Reviewed for accuracy by:
Jerry Johnson
Professor of Economics
    and Director of Center for Economic Education
University of Wisconsin-Eau Claire

David J. Whitehead
Chairman, Department of Economics,
    Geography, and Business Education
University of London

Library of Congress Number: 89-10463

1 2 3 4 5 6 7 8 9   93 92 91 90 89

Library of Congress Cataloging in Publication Data

Davis, Jim, 1940-
    London.
    (World cities)

    Summary: Explores the history, cultural heritage, demographics, geography, and economic and natural resources of London.
1. London (England)—Juvenile literature. [1. London (England)] I. Hawke, Sharryl Davis. II. Title. III. Series: Davis, Jim, 1940-   . World cities.
DA678.D38   1989   942.1   [B] [92]   89-10463
ISBN 0-8172-3027-0 (lib. bdg.)

Cover Photo: Arthur Threadgill

LONDON

WORLD CITIES

JAMES E. DAVIS
AND
SHARRYL DAVIS HAWKE

RAINTREE PUBLISHERS
Milwaukee

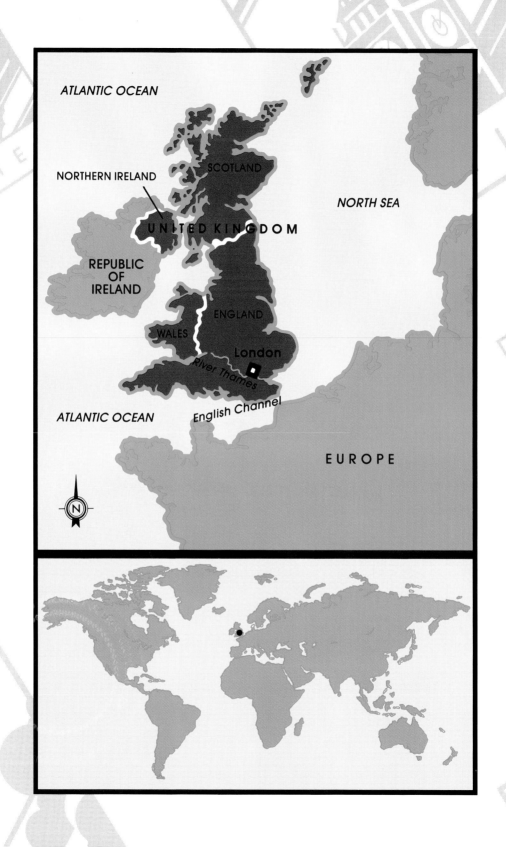

Contents

Introduction

When you think of London, you probably think of kings and queens, of rain and fog, of palaces and Parliament, of Sherlock Holmes and London Bridge.

But if a young visitor from London came to your class, what might he or she tell you about the city? He or she, no doubt, would tell you that the queen and her family live in London. It is foggy and rainy at times, but not as often as you might think. And yes, there are very large, old buildings where the royal family lives and where politicians carry on their work. He or she would also tell you that there are many famous people, not just characters from books, who have lived in London. Also, there have been several London Bridges, not just one.

You might learn of "Big Ben," the great bell that chimes every quarter hour in the clock tower rising from the Houses of Parliament. You would learn of the River Thames and how the city is built along its banks. You would be told how the city has circuses. A circus is the circular area formed where several streets intersect. The streets surrounding the circus approach from all directions, like spokes on a bicycle wheel. One of the most famous circuses is Piccadilly Circus. It is in the heart of downtown London and is surrounded by shops, restaurants, entertainment, and bright lights.

Your young visitor from London would probably describe a "typical day" as spent much like yours, in a

London is viewed from the dome of St. Paul's Cathedral.

school much like yours. In England, children are required to go to school from five until age sixteen. Primary schools are for children from five to eleven years old. Secondary schools are for students from eleven through sixteen or older.

After school in London, your visitor might get together with some friends in the schoolyard to play football. The English game of football is the game you may know as soccer. At home in the evening, your visitor would probably enjoy a meal with his or her family, do some homework, and watch television or a home video.

In England, as in the United States, families are smaller now. There may be just one or two children in the family. Your friend's mother and father may both work. Their work weeks are probably between thirty-five and forty hours a week. This may be just a little shorter than your parents' work week.

Where in the World is London?

London was once the largest city in the world. Though that title now belongs to Mexico City, London remains one of the top world cities. It is clearly the most important city in Great Britain and is, in fact, its capital. Great Britain is an island made up of three countries: England, Scotland, and Wales. Great Britain and North-

ern Ireland together form the United Kingdom.

If you look at at a map of Europe, you will see two large islands just north of France. The smaller island is Ireland; the larger one is Great Britain. Within Great Britain itself, Scotland lies in the northern part. Wales is located along the island's west coast. England, which is the largest of the three countries, makes up the rest of Great Britain.

To the east of Great Britain stretches the North Sea. This sea separates England from northern Europe. Directly south of Great Britain, between England and France, is a narrow water body known as the English Channel. This channel connects the Atlantic Ocean with the North Sea. You may have heard of athletes swimming across the English Channel. This channel, known for its cold, rough water and strong currents, has been a challenge for many swimmers.

In the southeast corner of England, there is a narrow spot where the English Channel flows into the North Sea. Just north of this, you will see a spot that looks like someone cut a nick in the coastline of England. That nick is the mouth of the River Thames (pronounced temz). The River Thames has been a working river for many generations. Farther inland, the river is too shallow for big merchant ships, but the deep waters at the Port of London make this area ideal as an important trade district. From this port, Britain carries on trade with the rest of the world.

Moving west up the Thames for 45 miles (72 kilometers), London unfolds before your eyes. Ships have been sailing up the River Thames to London for almost two thousand years. Remember, the United States celebrated its two hundreth birthday in 1976. Think about how much older London is than New York City. Today, the Port of London is not as busy as it was in the past. During World War II, the dockyards of central London were destroyed. Dockyard activity then began developing farther downriver. Recently, the deserted dockyards of London have come alive again. Small businesses have developed. Offices and stylish new homes are now being built here.

Both New York and London are located on major rivers. Both are large cities that are important world business and trade centers. They are also top entertainment capitals and important political centers. But London is very different from New York in many ways. Let's explore London.

Tower Bridge is one of many bridges that span the River Thames.

How the City Began

Long ago, during the Ice Age, ice covered much of the land in Europe just as it did in the United States. Only a few thousand people lived in Britain then. They lived as hunters, fishermen, and gatherers and used tools made of stone and bone.

When the ice melted, the amount of water in the North Sea increased. It increased so much that part of what had been dry land was now under the water. This is how Great Britain became an island and the English Channel was formed. But despite the channel, people still came from Europe to Britain. Between 5000 and 3000 B.C., these people introduced farming and farming tools. Some of these tools were made of bronze and later of iron.

The Celts and the Romans

About 500 B.C., a new group of farmers and warriors came from Central Europe to settle throughout Britain. They were called the Celts. A site along the River Thames about 45 miles (72 km) from where it joins the North Sea seemed like a good site for a fortress. The Celts built one there and called the area *Lyndin*, which means "waterside fortress."

The Romans first came to Britain about 55 B.C. At that time, soldiers led by Julius Caesar came just to explore the island. The Romans came again around A.D. 43. This time they came to conquer and rule over the people who lived there. They set up a military base in Lyndin, which they began call-

ing Londinium. Roman laws were introduced to the people who lived there. Queen Boudicca of the Celts used her armies to try to force the Romans to leave. But it was no use; the Romans planned to stay.

The Romans built many forts throughout Britain, but Londinium became especially important. They built a huge wall around it, enclosing over 300 acres (121 hectares). They also built the first London Bridge. It was made of wood, and the Roman army used it to cross the Thames.

Today, the central part of London is built upon many of the old Roman buildings and roads, including the Roman wall. In the 1940s, during World War II, many of the buildings in London were destroyed. Beneath these destroyed buildings, the remains of the Roman city were found. Many Roman artifacts are in the Museum of London today.

The Roman city of Londinium lasted for over three hundred years. Then, in A.D. 410, the emperor of the Roman Empire ordered the Roman troops to leave Britain. The soldiers were needed back in Rome to help defend the city from barbarians. As a result, Londinium, which had grown into the most important trade center north of the Alps, was deserted by the Romans.

Part of an ancient wall built by Roman soldiers still stands near Tower Hill.

Other Tribes and Traders Come To London

Soon other tribes from northern Europe came to eastern Britain. They were the Angles, the Saxons, and the Jutes. The Saxons settled around London and finally took over the city. The Vikings, who were traders and fighters from Scandinavia, were the next group to overrun London. The Vikings were later forced from the city by King Alfred. This king then rebuilt London and chose it as his capital city for ruling Britain.

A city as old as the city of London really has many beginnings—first as a fishing village; next, as a military base for the Romans in Britain; last as a trading center for the Saxons and later the Vikings. Under King Alfred,

London became the capital of Britain. King Alfred pursued peace for his kingdom. He was also interested in education. He established the first school to teach his people how to read and write. At his request, important books were translated from Latin to English. He also set up the first government for the city of London.

William the Conqueror's London

Perhaps modern London truly began after William the Conqueror of Normandy invaded Britain in 1066. Under the Normans, beginning with King William and for the next several hundred years, London grew as a center of business and finance.

The White Tower was built by invading Norman soldiers. From this fortress, the Normans ruled over London's Saxon population.

©Lee C. Hauenstein

During this time, guilds, or city companies, began to form. Each guild was developed around a single trade, such as making clothes, shoes, or tools, or working at the docks. Each guild had a special guildhall that was located in the part of the city where the trade was practiced. Each guild trained its own workers. People learning a trade were called apprentices. An apprentice usually trained for seven years. Then the apprentice had to pass a difficult exam before he could become a full member of the guild. The guilds were important in government because they elected members to the council that governed the city.

In eleventh-century London, the homes were mostly made of wood. They were heated by fires, and smoke escaped from a small hole in the thatched roofs. There were no glass windows. Instead, wooden shutters were used. As you can imagine, houses and other buildings often caught on fire. Only the wealthy people of London lived in homes built of stone.

Some important buildings were constructed during this time. The style of architecture was grand. While William was king, a section of the Tower of London was built. Its central section was called the White Tower. While Henry III was king, Westminster Abbey, a very large and famous church, was built. It replaced the pre-

The Inns of Court have been home to London's legal profession since the 1400s. A present-day barrister, or lawyer, is pictured.

vious Westminster that had been built by King Edward the Confessor. Lawyers in the city formed groups and rented space in the grand Inns of Court. Originally, these inns were built as residences for knights. Eventually the inns became similar to colleges; law students both lived and studied in them. Many of these buildings are still standing in London.

Fourteenth-Century London

In the fourteenth century, most Londoners made their living by buying and selling goods. Early in the day, the city was filled with the sounds of horse-pulled carts making their way to market. Every evening the bells at the gates of the city rang to warn that the gates would soon be closed.

London's streets were narrow and made of cobbled stone. A gutter ran down the middle of each street, carrying water run-off. These gutters were also used for dumping household wastes. To make matters worse, pigs and other animals roamed freely. So the streets were smelly and polluted. The River Thames was also polluted. It was used both as a place to dump garbage and as a source of drinking water. With these unhealthy conditions, disease spread easily. Many people died during outbreaks of the plague, a contagious disease carried by rats. One particularly bad outbreak of the plague, called the Black Death, began in 1348. By the time the disease quieted down, almost one-fourth of Europe's population had died.

Shops were small with a workroom in the back. Above the shops were apartments three or four stories high that often hung over the streets. The houses and shops were made of wood and had pointed roofs.

Shakespeare's London

In spite of wars, political confusion, and disease, London continued to grow and prosper in the fifteenth and sixteenth centuries. It was also a time of change. During the reign of Henry VIII, England broke away from the Roman Catholic Church. One reason for the break was that the pope refused to approve of Henry's divorce and remarriage. Henry wished to divorce Catherine of Aragon, the first of his six wives, because she had not given him a son. To provide an heir to the throne, Henry wished to remarry. After his break with the Church, Henry VIII established the Church of England. He also had Parliament pass

a law that named the king, not the pope, as head of this church.

Henry's daughter Elizabeth eventually became Queen Elizabeth I and reigned for forty-five years, from the end of the sixteenth century into the early seventeenth. During her reign, England became a world power. She defeated the great Spanish army, and many of her knights sailed to the New World to claim colonies for England.

William Shakespeare, the great playwright, lived during the reign of Queen Elizabeth I and wrote about life in London during this time. If you could go back and walk the streets of London with Shakespeare, he would show you the Globe Theatre in Southwark.

This etching shows London as it appeared during the lifetime of playwright William Shakespeare.

Many of Shakespeare's tragedies were performed in this theater, and he also acted there. Also, he would probably introduce you to his friends and fellow playwrights, Christopher Marlowe and Ben Jonson. The works of these men, as well as that of other writers, poets, and scholars, thrived during Elizabeth's reign.

If you could walk the narrow streets of London with Shakespeare, you would notice that many of the houses and buildings were made of brick with wooden frames. Roofs were made of tile or lead. The houses were heated with coal instead of wood, and chimneys were added later to help the smoke escape. You would certainly notice the pollution. It was caused by the smoke from chimneys mingling with fog from the river. This problem grew as small industries increased. These industries burned fires most of the day.

In Shakespeare's London, people used the Thames as a source of water. Water also came from city wells. But by Shakespeare's time, these wells were polluted. Fresh water had to be brought into the city from springs in outlying areas. As London's population boomed, the demand for water increased. Often, there just wasn't enough clean water to meet everyone's needs.

The Plague and the Fire

Shakespeare's time, which mainly took place during Elizabeth I's reign, was a period of growth, power, and success. Soon after this time, however, London faced two severe setbacks. The first was another bout with the plague in 1665. This final outbreak, known as the Great Plague, was so severe that it killed one-third of the city's people.

Just as London was recovering from this tragedy, a huge fire broke out in the city. This fire, which is called the Great Fire of 1666, started at the city's

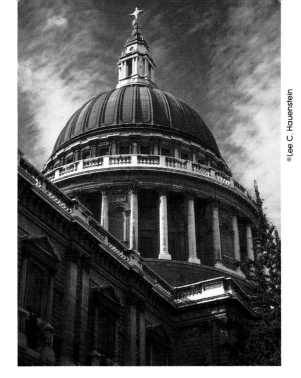

St. Paul's Cathedral, burned in the Great Fire of 1666, was redesigned by Sir Christopher Wren.

center. It burned for four days and destroyed almost everything. Despite the destruction it caused, the fire may have helped wipe out the plague once and for all.

With events such as these, it is easy to see how London's history represents a series of beginnings. It also shows the people's determination. After the fire, the city was rebuilt. A young architect and inventor, Sir Christopher Wren, drew up plans for the city's reconstruction. While he designed more than 150 churches, he is best known for redesigning St. Paul's Cathedral, which had also burned in the fire. Wren's style was unique and inspired a large group of followers.

Growth to 1900

At the beginning of the eighteenth century, Anne became queen of England. Queen Anne's London was the city of the famous architects Christopher Wren and Inigo Jones. Already it was one of the most important seaports in Europe and had a population of over half a million people. Yet it continued to grow in size and in importance. London's population growth was especially active as people from other countries poured into England. These immigrants came to England with the hope that they could improve their lives.

Queen Anne left no heirs to the throne. Although she had had six children (one of whom died at birth), none of them outlived her. Following her short reign from 1702-1714, Anne's cousin George from Germany became king.

London as a Growing Center for World Trade

During the time of King George, Britain had many colonies in North America. These colonies helped Britain become an important center for world trade. The colonies bought products that they needed from England. They sold raw materials such as cotton and tobacco to England.

Many jobs in London had to do with sea trade. London needed shipbuilders, dockworkers, carpenters, and rope-and-sailmakers. The merchants who owned ships were considered among the most important people in London. Trade helped London become a growing, prosperous city. As a result, many people had work to do and money to spend.

Ben Franklin Visits London

In the North American colonies, Ben Franklin, a young printer from Philadelphia, wondered what life was like in London. In 1724, he made a trip to London to see for himself and to learn more about printing. Compared with London, Philadelphia seemed like a village. London was big and old; it had narrow streets and many people, many of whom were poor.

Franklin found a place to live in a working-class neighborhood near St. Paul's Cathedral and soon got a job at Palmer's Printing House. He found London an exciting place. He enjoyed going to plays at the Theatre Royal on

Admirers surround Benjamin Franklin after one of his trips to London. While in London, Franklin began using a sedan chair, a popular type of transportation.

This etching shows eighteenth-century silversmiths creating silver utensils. The artist used letters to mark the different steps in the process.

Drury Lane and seeing the opera performed in the Haymarket. Like Londoners, Franklin enjoyed cricket matches in Chelsea and "Punch and Judy" puppet shows on the sidewalks in town.

In the London that Franklin visited, shopkeepers and craftspeople were always busy. Sometimes shops opened as early as 7:00 A.M. and did not close until 10:00 P.M. There were shoemakers, potters, glassblowers, tailors, silversmiths, and blacksmiths. Many people worked seventy to ninety hours a week.

London was full of marketplaces. Every day, people who lived in and around London came to the marketplaces to sell food and supplies. Butter, cheese, and corn came from Suffolk. Turkeys and chickens came from Norfolk. Fish came from the fishing villages in southern England, and coal came from Newcastle. Markets for the different products were set up throughout London. In Covent Garden, there were fruit and vegetable markets. Hay for the horses could be found at Haymarket. The biggest market was at Smithfield where ham, beef, and lamb were sold by butchers. There were also peddlers who traveled up and down the streets to sell coal, matches, milk, or pies.

The children of London were busy working, too. The boys cleaned stables and chimneys, or made buttons and delivered messages. The girls

Hampton Court Palace was partially redesigned by Sir Christopher Wren. Wren's style influenced London's architects for many years.

F.E. Jenkins/JIG

washed laundry, worked as maids for wealthy people, or did sewing and wound silk. Many children, especially those from poor families, had to help their families by working. There was no time to go to school. For many people, living conditions were crowded and work was hard. Diseases such as smallpox, typhus, and flu spread quickly and killed many people.

During the eighteenth century, the architecture of London took on a new style called Georgian, after the Kings George I, II, III, and IV. Architects designed beautiful churches and homes using arches and rows of columns. Inigo Jones's style, imported from Italy, greatly influenced the Georgian period. Georgian style was also popular in the American colonies, where the design was later changed somewhat.

The Industrial Revolution Changes London

Manufacturing also began in London during the eighteenth century. Manufacturing involves workers using machines to make products. Before this, people had made goods by hand in their homes or in small shops. But people working together using machines in "manufactories" were able to turn out many more products. Machines included a pumping engine that ran on steam, a large, heavy hammer that also used steam, and a spinning machine that ran on water power. Many other machines were invented in England during this period.

This wide use of machines in manufactories ushered in the Industrial Revolution. This revolution began in Great Britain in the 1700s. With its many colonies, Great Britain was supplied the raw materials it needed and had ready markets for the products it manufactured. The revolution brought both positive effects such as prosperity and new inventions, and negative effects such as terrible working conditions. It changed London and the rest of Great Britain just as it would later change America and the rest of the world. From its origin, the revolution spread to the rest of Europe and North America by the mid-1800s.

Queen Victoria's London

In 1837, at the age of eighteen, Victoria became queen of England. Until she was eleven, she did not know that she would one day be queen. When she found out, as history tells it, she

This statue at Windsor Castle honors Queen Victoria. During her reign, the British Empire reached the height of its growth.

Samuel B. Saylor/JIG

said, "I will be good." She was right. Victoria was a hard-working, decisive, and effective queen. Her dedication gave the people new respect for the throne. Her reign also brought England to the height of its industrialization. And as industrialization continued to grow, wealth continued to follow it.

But the very source of wealth was also a major problem—especially in London. The rapid growth of the industries and the population created terrible living and working conditions. This dark side of Victorian London was the setting for Charles Dickens's stories. Dickens, a famous British writer, wrote about life in London, especially about children in the slums. You may have heard of some of his famous stories such as *Oliver Twist* and *Great Expectations*.

Slums—sections of cities where poor families lived in crowded, unhealthy conditions—sprang up in most big cities. As more people moved to the cities looking for jobs in factories, the slums grew. It was during the Victorian era that public leaders such as Lord Shaftesbury began to pay more attention to the slums and their horrid conditions. Shaftesbury, as well as men such as William Booth, tried to

The crowded and unhealthy slums became a way of life during London's Industrial Revolution.

Bettmann/Hulton

Through his novels, British writer Charles Dickens spoke out against the dark side of Victorian London.

make things better. Booth, an English preacher, began an organization to help the poor. This organization eventually became the Salvation Army.

The poor people also tried to help themselves. They knew that going to school and getting an education was very valuable. Having an education could mean a better way of life for them. Many schools were built during this time, and children who had never gone to school before began to learn to read and write.

You can see that although the eighteenth and nineteenth centuries were full of promise and advances for London, there were also many problems for the growing city.

London in the Twentieth Century

When Queen Victoria died in 1901, the British Empire—Britain and its colonies—was still growing. Victoria's eldest son was crowned King Edward VII. Edward proved himself a smart and diplomatic ruler. This became clear when he helped develop friendly relations with France. The new ally became very important during World War I, which began in 1914. Britain and its allies—France and the United States—triumphed in the conflict.

London Between the Wars

During the decades between World War I and World War II, London and the rest of Britain were led by the first Labour government. At its head was James Ramsay MacDonald. As a member of the Labour Party, MacDonald represented the interests and concerns of the workers. During this period, popular King Edward VIII voluntarily gave up the throne to marry an American woman named Wallis Simpson. The government, the Church of England, and many British subjects did not approve of the marriage because Simpson had been divorced. King Edward could not marry her and remain king of England. Edward's brother George then became king. George then named Edward the Duke of Windsor.

London's Bravest Hour

To many people, World War II is considered London's hardest time.

But it was also London's bravest time. Britain entered World War II when Nazi Germany invaded Poland in 1939. The war lasted until 1945; the United States joined in toward the end of 1941.

Winston Churchill was prime minister of Britain during the war. His forceful, determined qualities were very important to the British people—especially when London was bombed repeatedly. The city became a central target for German air-raids between 1940 and 1941. Many sections of the city were damaged or totally destroyed during the bombings which took place at night.

Because of the bombings, many Londoners slept in special air-raid shelters or on the platforms of subway stations every night. Can you imagine sleeping in places like that for months at a time and waking up every morning to see more of the city in ruins? As always, the people endured. Winston Churchill admired this about the people of his country. He was proud of what he called "the tough fiber of the Londoners."

During the war, King George VI and Queen Elizabeth stayed at Buckingham Palace. They did not desert their city. Winston Churchill's office during the war was under the Treasury building, whose foundation was 30 feet (9 meters) underground.

When the war was finally over, thirty thousand Londoners had been killed and fifty thousand had been injured. The damage to the city was devastating. In central London, nine out of ten homes were either destroyed or damaged. In the old section called the City, one-third of the buildings were destroyed. Churches and guildhalls were ruined throughout London. Miraculously, Wren's St. Paul's Cathedral was not destroyed. It was only slightly damaged.

A Time to Rebuild, Again

London was in ruins, but it had been rebuilt many times. Before the war was even over, Sir Patrick Abercrombie had written up plans for

Winston Churchill was Britain's prime minister during World War II. Churchill vowed that his country would "never surrender" to the Nazis.

London's reconstruction. He believed that this was an opportunity to change some of the things that were wrong with the city's design. He wanted to improve such things as old, unsuitable housing, unorganized road systems, improper location of industries, too few open spaces, and no real sense of city planning.

Abercrombie's plan included organizing city streets into "ring roads," or "circuses," and moving many of London's industries to other locations. His plan was accepted, but it took time and money to do the rebuilding. By 1951, however, over forty thousand new homes and flats, or apartments, had been built. Places that had been leveled by bombs now served as foun-

A Londoner stands in the rubble of her home after a Nazi bombing raid.

UPI/Bettmann Newsphotos

dations for a few skyscrapers. Many of the historic buildings that had been damaged, such as Guildhall and St. Paul's Cathedral, had to be repaired.

During the 1950s, London was set aside as a "smokeless zone." According to Abercrombie's plan, most of the city's smoke-causing industries had to

Plans for London's reorganization included circular intersections called circuses. Picadilly Circus, seen here, is one of the most famous.

move elsewhere. Also, London's docks and related industries were not rebuilt in the same place after the war. They were moved a little farther down the Thames.

After World War II, Britain adopted governmental changes to help bring about social reform. These reforms included payments to people who were unable to find jobs, health insurance that provided almost free public medical care, and monthly pensions for the elderly.

Queen Elizabeth II's London

In 1952, the present queen of England, Elizabeth II, was crowned. She and her husband, Philip, have four

Queen Elizabeth II is Britain's reigning monarch. Elizabeth became queen in 1952.

British Information Services

children. From youngest to oldest, they are: Edward, Andrew, Anne, and Charles. Charles, the Prince of Wales, is destined to be the next king of England.

By the 1960s, the people of London and all of Britain enjoyed an increase in their standard of living. They were making more money and were able to have things, such as washing machines, freezers, and televisions sets, that made life easier and better.

In 1965, London, London County, and parts of surrounding counties joined together to form Greater London. It has an area of 620 square miles (1,605 sq. km) and a population of almost eight million. Until 1986, Greater London was governed by the Greater London Council. This council no longer exists. Its duties were taken over by the governments of the city's thirty-two boroughs (sections) and the government of the City of London.

In the 1970s, London and Britain experienced a period of inflation, when prices everywhere were going up. When the oil-producing countries of the Middle East forced up the price of oil in 1973, matters got worse. Prices continued to rise and so did unemployment.

By the late 1970s, the economy turned around again for London and Great Britain. The computer industry took hold and the banking industry

Buckingham Palace has been the official residence of British royalty since 1837.

experienced new growth. Continued growth in these areas means new jobs for people in the future. It also means a different type of trade for Britain. Instead of exporting steel, cars, textiles, and engineering products, Britain is now selling computer products and oil, which was discovered in the North Sea.

There is a sense of well-being in London these days. People are making more money, working fewer hours, and living longer than at any time in London's past. Margaret Thatcher, elected prime minister in 1979, was the first woman to hold this position. Although she has faced difficult problems such as inflation and high unemployment, Thatcher has been a leader dedicated to the people.

A recent trend in construction has given the city quite a different look. There are more skyscrapers and more buildings of concrete and glass. Not everyone is pleased with these new buildings, and housing is still a problem. But the new look represents a new and modern London—a London that must settle in and rub shoulders with historic London.

Royalty and the British Empire

One striking feature of London is its royalty. London has been home to kings, queens, princes, and princesses for twelve centuries. London was also the center of the British Empire—an empire that was vast, strong, and influenced the entire world. There was a saying, "The sun never sets on the British Empire." This was true. Because Britain had territories all over the world, at any given time, it was daytime in at least one of its territories.

London's Royalty

There is royalty in London because Britain began as a monarchy long ago. In a monarchy, the leader, called a monarch, is not elected the way the people of the United States elect a president. A monarch becomes a leader because he or she is born into a family that is already ruling. Today's Queen Elizabeth became queen when her father, George VI, died. Prince Charles will become king when his mother, Elizabeth, dies. When the king or queen has no children, then the leadership usually goes to a niece, nephew, or other relative.

King Egbert was the first person to rule England as a monarch. He was king of only England; Scotland and Wales had separate rulers. Later, Wales became part of Great Britain, and in the early 1700s, Scotland also became part of Great Britain.

The power of the monarch has always been challenged. First, the nobles tried to have a say in how to run things and to control the monarch. Later, members of Parliament, the governing body of Britain, wanted different groups, such as merchants, to be heard and to have importance. Parliament is the group of people that governs Britain much like Congress governs the United States. Parliament is made up of the monarch, the House of Commons, and the House of Lords. Members of the House of Commons are elected by the people in a general election. Many members of the House

During his reign, King Charles I clashed with Parliament over the power of the monarch. These clashes led to civil war in 1642 and Charles's execution in 1649.

FPG

of Lords inherit their positions; others are chosen by the monarch. The prime minister, who heads Parliament, is chosen by its members.

A successful challenge to the monarchy came in the mid-1600s. At that time, Parliament's role was growing, and it demanded more power. When King Charles I resisted, he was executed. The monarchy was abolished but was restored about ten years later. But since then, most monarchs have not tried to control Parliament. Britain's kings and queens "reign but do not rule" the country. Instead, Britain is led by the prime minister and the members of Parliament.

The Sun Never Sets

The British Empire had its beginnings long ago. Britain's first overseas colony was in Ireland, founded in 1171. In the 1400s and 1500s, Britain had little success in establishing colonies in the New World. But its trading companies were so successful at buying and selling in the New World, that eventually Britain was able to settle in Virginia, Maryland, New England, Bermuda, Barbados, and the Leeward Islands. In the mid-1600s, Britain captured Spanish Jamaica and New Amsterdam (now New York, New Jersey, and Delaware). Pennsylvania and the Carolinas were peaceably established as British colonies.

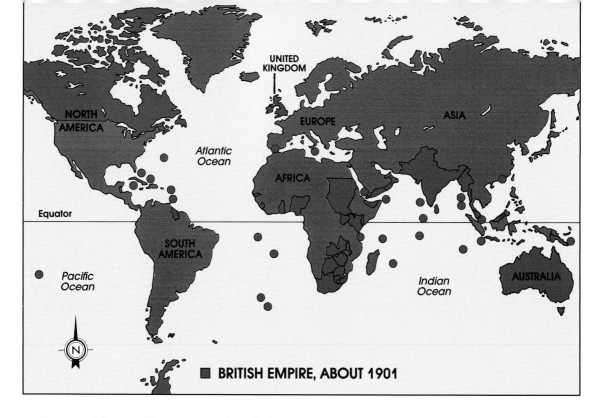

UNITED KINGDOM

NORTH AMERICA

EUROPE

ASIA

Atlantic Ocean

AFRICA

Equator

SOUTH AMERICA

Pacific Ocean

Indian Ocean

AUSTRALIA

N

■ BRITISH EMPIRE, ABOUT 1901

Through its trading companies, Britain established interests in India in the early 1600s and West Africa in the late 1600s. West and South Africa were rich in ivory and diamonds; India had wonderful teas and spices. Later, in the 1700s, Britain's North American colonies became upset with British rule. They did not want to be taxed on items that they had to buy, especially if they were not represented in Parliament. The American Revolution resulted, and the colonists' Continental Army won the war. The United States was established as an independent nation, no longer under British rule.

The British Empire continued to expand to Australia, New Zealand, South and Central Africa, and islands

The British Empire reached the height of its power between 1837 and 1901. Its domain spanned the globe. Because of its many colonies and dominions, the sun truly did not set on the British Empire.

in the Pacific. For much of the 1800s, Britain was the most powerful country in the world. As the empire expanded, it became harder to rule because it included so many people in so many places. It wasn't easy to meet everyone's needs or keep everyone happy. Many reforms, or changes, were taking place in the colonies. By the late 1800s and early 1900s, Britain began giving its colonies dominion status, or equal status, instead of keeping them as colonies. Canada was among the first of these dominions. It is now an independent country.

Every year, the queen addresses the House of Lords as part of the official opening of Parliament.

Britain and many of its former colonies maintain close ties. Here, the queen reviews the troops in the Bahamas.

Taking Apart an Empire

In the early 1900s, the British Empire gradually became known as the British Commonwealth of Nations. As Britain continued to give more colonies their independence, it had to adapt to a different role in the world.

After 1949, the British Commonwealth of Nations became known as the Commonwealth of Nations, with the queen as its head. Through this association, Britain still has ties with its former territories. Little remains of the once rich and powerful empire that included one-fifth of the world's people. Although the empire no longer exists, the tradition of royalty continues.

Places in the City

London's history is both the story of a great city and the story of the British Empire. So when you see London, you see a city rich with hundreds of years of history. In touring the city, its history comes alive. Imagine touring London. Walking is the best way to tour, but don't worry, many parks and gardens will offer rest along the way. You can also take the underground, or subway, or ride on the bright red double-decker buses.

Some things about the city will be almost the same as when Ben Franklin visited London in the 1700s. Other things will be very different. As you arrive in London and come into the city, you will at once notice London's grandeur, the old and new together.

The City—with a Capital "C"

The oldest part of London is a section called the City, with a capital "C." Although it covers only 1 square mile (2.6 sq. km) the city brims with many famous places to see. It is the true historic center of London, and the site of the beginning of London. Beneath the City are the ruins of the Roman city Londinium. Remains of the wall that the Romans built in the third century still stand.

The Tower of London is one of the most famous buildings to see. It is actually a group of sixteen buildings. The first to be built was the central White Tower for William the Conqueror in 1067. It served as a lookout tower over the River Thames to protect the city from invasion. Other monarchs added more towers and a ring of deep water, called a moat, around it. A section of the Tower was sometimes used as a palace, another was used as a prison, and another was a zoo. Part of the Tower called the Jewel House is the place where the crown jewels are kept, including St. Edward's crown which was made for Charles II in the 1600s. This crown was last worn by Elizabeth II when she was crowned queen in 1953.

While at the Tower, you will notice the guards. The guards, called Yeomen Warders, wear colorful costumes. These traditional costumes are the

The Tower of London is popular with tourists.

uniforms of five hundred years ago. Also while you are at the Tower, you will notice the black ravens flocking around. According to legend, if the ravens should leave the Tower, it would fall and so would the British Empire.

Near the Tower, you will see the Tower Bridge. This is one of fifteen bridges that stretch across the River Thames in London. This bridge was built in 1894 and designed to go with the Tower. There is a walkway across a section of the bridge that gives you a wonderful view up and down the river.

A little farther upriver from the Tower Bridge stands London Bridge. London Bridge is London's first and most-famous bridge. Over the years, this bridge has been replaced many times. The first bridge and at least two others were made of wood. The children's song "London Bridge Is Falling Down" was written about one of these wooden bridges. The present bridge is made of stone. Before this bridge was built, at least two others were built of stone. When the second stone bridge was dismantled, the stones were shipped to Lake Havasu City, Arizona. There, the bridge was rebuilt. It opened as a tourist attraction in 1971.

A Yeoman Warder, one of the Tower's guards, gives visitors a history of the site (right).

38

As you walk west of the Tower Bridge and the Tower of London, you will see a tall, thin column. This is the Monument. It was built in 1667 as a memorial to the Great Fire of 1666. The Monument is 202 feet (61 m) tall. It also stands 202 feet (61 m) from where the fire started on Pudding Lane. A spiral staircase inside winds 311 stairs to the top. This climb, which offers a great view from the top, is a favorite of Londoners and visitors.

As you walk north and west from the Monument, you will spot the Mansion House, where the lord mayor of London lives. The Royal Exchange, where the buying and selling of stock began in the 1600s, is also here. The Royal Exchange is like the stock market on New York City's Wall Street. A few blocks north of the Royal Exchange you will see Guildhall on the left. Parts of this beautiful building are just the way they were in the 1400s. This building serves as the headquarters for the people who govern the City. Inside, you can visit the Great Hall, the Guildhall Library, and the Clock Museum.

If you then turn around and head southwest, you will see the majestic dome of St. Paul's Cathedral. This church is one of the city's most famous.

The interior of St. Paul's Cathedral is breathtaking (left).

It was designed by Sir Christopher Wren after the first St. Paul's was destroyed in the Great Fire of 1666. Inside, you can see the beautiful dome, the High Altar of marble and oak, and the tombs of Sir Christopher Wren and others.

If you continue southwest after your visit to St. Paul's, you will be on Fleet Street. This street was originally used to cross the Fleet River. But the river was filled in and covered with cobblestones in the 1700s because it was so polluted. Today, Fleet Street is famous for its many newspaper offices.

Guildhall has been the seat of the City government since the 1400s.

© Arthur Threadgill

The Palace of Westminster is the meeting place of the Houses of Parliament.

Westminster and the West End

In the early days, the City and Westminster were separate villages. As activity between these two sections increased, London grew to include both villages. The road connecting these sections is called the Strand. The Strand is still a famous London street. In Westminster, along the banks of the Thames, you will see the huge and sprawling Houses of Parliament, also called the Palace of Westminster. For several hundred years, this was where the English Parliament met and where the king or queen lived. Today, Parliament meets here, but the queens and kings no longer live here. (Buckingham Palace is now the home of British royalty.) Victoria Tower is one of two well-known towers rising from the Houses of Parliament structure. Victoria Tower is the largest tower, but the tower on the east corner is the most famous. This clock tower is known as Big Ben, although the name

Big Ben rings the hour from Victoria Tower (left). Westminster Abbey has been the site of every coronation ceremony since 1066 (above).

really belongs to the tower's great bell. Big Ben, which first rang out in 1859, chimes each hour.

Across from the Houses of Parliament is Westminster Abbey. The Abbey is a well-known site in British history. Since the time of William the Conqueror, England's kings and queens have been crowned here. A church has stood on this site for over one thousand years. The original church was an abbey built in St.

Peter's honor. Officially, the Abbey's name is still the Collegiate Church of St. Peter. This church has been rebuilt, restored, and added to since the eighth century.

Farther west you will see Buckingham Palace. The royal family has lived in this palace since Queen Victoria's time. A little northeast of this palace is St. James's Palace where kings and queens lived one hundred years ago. The ceremony of the Changing of the Guard here is something you won't want to miss.

From here you catch a bus or the underground back to the center of the West End. This is Piccadilly Circus, the heart of downtown London. This lively area is known for its many shops, art galleries, restaurants, and theaters. The West End, in fact, is home to some of England's major theaters. In the center of all of this activity stands the statue of Eros (the Greek god of love). This statue is actually the Angel of Christian Charity, as named by the artist who created it. The Londoners, however, continue

Members of the Royal Guard march daily in front of St. James's Palace.

©Arthur Threadgill

At Speaker's Corner in Hyde Park, any person can address the crowd on any topic (above). Hyde Park offers recreation all year round, as seen in this winter photo (right).

to call the statue Eros, and it is by this name the statue is best known.

Hyde Park, Kensington Gardens, and More

After the bustle of the city, you might want to take a bus to a quieter place in London. South and west of here is Mayfair, a very fashionable part of London. There you will see the open spaces of Hyde Park and Kensington Gardens. These two huge parks offer a beautiful, peaceful setting for walking, swimming, horseback riding,

At the National Gallery, a piece of artwork is cleaned and restored.

and other outdoor activities. The huge Serpentine Lake stretches between the two parks. Rowing on the Serpentine and strolling along its banks are particularly popular pastimes.

There are many more wonderful churches, houses, arches, parks, and squares to see in London. There are also some wonderful museums, espe-cially the British Museum, the Natural History Museum, the Victoria and Albert Museum, and the National Gallery. London is full of places to see and things to do. It is a city with a very rich history. Samuel Johnson, an English writer who lived in London during the 1700s, used to say, "If you are tired of London, you are tired of life."

WORLD

CITIES

What Makes London Work?

When you look at Britain on a map, you may wonder why a little spot in the southeast corner of the country could have grown so important. After all, Britain is an island. Most people think of islands as places away from the world—places of isolation.

But look again. The English Channel is only 21 miles (34 km) wide, and the island is not that far off the coast of the rest of northern Europe. Because it was surrounded by water, ships could easily get to Britain. But being surrounded by water was only part of the country's attraction. Ships also needed protection and quiet harbors where loading and unloading could take place. Britain had these, too.

The River Thames

The River Thames is probably the single most important feature in London's development. Remember, London is situated about 45 miles (72 km) upriver from the mouth of the Thames. Here the river is deep and wide enough to move great numbers of ships in and out of London docks.

This setting was perfect for developing trade. But with whom was London going to trade? Britain had established a number of trading companies, many based in London. These companies set out to develop trade networks all over the world. Their ships traveled to Russia, the Mediterranean, Java, India, West Africa, and North

The busy Thames docks were rebuilt after World War II. The docks continue to be important to Britain because the country must import many goods.

America. Through their trade, the companies supplied Britain with many raw goods. They also became very powerful in some of these foreign places. Eventually, Britain established colonies in many of these places. This is how the empire began.

Many goods were made into useful products and exported back to the colonies or other countries. For example, iron was made into nails, pots, and tools. Raw cotton was used to make cloth and clothing. Furs were made into hats. The British used other goods such as tobacco and tea for themselves.

By collecting taxes, or duties, on products, London and all of Britain continued to grow and prosper. Of course, there were other ports in Britain, but London was by far the largest and the busiest. During this time, more than three-fourths of the shipping activity took place in the London dockyards.

Trade is what made London work in the past, and the River Thames made that possible. The docks and related industries have since moved downriver. But London now serves as a financial center for most of the trade industry.

London's Changing Industries

Following World War II, it took almost twenty-five years for London to rebuild. During that time, Britain witnessed its decline as a world trading power. In the past twenty years, however, many industries with headquarters in London have modernized and now compete favorably in the world market. New factories have been built. Modern machines now produce chemicals, oil products, electronics, and scientific instruments. Britain was a pioneer in the computer industry and continues to have one of the largest computer industries in the world.

Britain now offers many services, rather than products, to other countries. These services include banking and insurance, scientific and technical information and expertise, and tourism. London is the center of all of these activities. The tourist industry in particular has always been important to London. Recently it has grown rapidly because it is now easier and cheaper for people to travel than it once was. More than twelve million tourists visit Britain yearly. London is by far its most important tourist city.

A flock of pigeons nearly buries this pair of visitors at Trafalgar Square.

©Arthur Threadgill

Working to Take Care of People

London has worked to take care of its people through every hardship: the plague, the Great Fire, World War II, the depression of the 1930s, and the inflation of the 1970s. In 1947, Britain made social changes that were designed to help its people. Public services such as medical care were set up. Public housing projects were built, providing better living conditions for many of Britain's poor people. All of these actions helped the people of London, just as they helped all of Britain.

Forty percent of Britain's women work. The government has tried to help their families with day-care and other needs. The government has also tried to improve the standing of ethnic minorities in London and the rest of Britain.

The underground transportation system, known as "the tube," is used by many Londoners for the ride to and from work.

©Arthur Threadgill

Transportation Linking London

The best way to see London is to walk. But the city has expanded so much in size that it's often too far to walk. Fortunately, several types of transportation are available.

London's underground transportation system is one method of travel. This system—"the tube" as Londoners call it—is made up of nine routes that travel throughout the city. Except for very short distances, the underground is also the fastest way to travel in London. Most Londoners use the tube to get to and from work.

A fleet of London taxis, known as "black cabs," crowds the approach to Buckingham Palace. These cabs are an expensive means of travel.

The city bus lines also are very convenient, especially for short trips. The bus lines are even better at covering London than is the underground. But the trips are slower. There are also the famous London "black cabs," a comfortable but expensive way to travel.

The railway system in and out of London has been important for the growth of suburbs. The rails are a fast, convenient way to get to and from the city. Many trains are electric; others are high-speed diesel trains.

Everything Money Can Buy

Shopping in London is a wonderful treat. The merchants of London have interesting ways of selling and displaying things for sale. And, of course, they are known for their good taste.

The best, most expensive places to shop in London are Piccadilly, Regent Street, Knightsbridge, and Kensington. One of the most famous stores in the world is Harrods in Knightsbridge. It was established in the late 1800s and is full of fascinating things to look at and to buy. It also includes a theater ticket office, a bank, a beauty shop, and a veterinarian's office. More moderate places to shop include Oxford Street and the Strand.

London is well known for its street markets such as Petticoat Lane and Covent Garden. There are also many speciality shops in London that sell china and glass, linens and woolens, desserts and cheeses, perfumes and jewelry, and books and stationery.

Sports and Pastimes

Londoners are enjoying more leisure time than ever before. If they have the space, they enjoy gardening.

At Harrods, the famous Knightsbridge department store, shoppers can find everything from crystal to woolens.

50

They also enjoy getting out of the city to fish, which is very popular with the British. Recently, walking and jogging have also become popular. Other sports, such as tennis, squash, golf, horse racing, and horseback riding are also important.

Team sports are also popular. Of all team sports, football (which Americans call soccer) is the favorite in London. Each year, the football season ends with championships in May. Tickets for this popular playoff are difficult to obtain. Cricket is another popular game. This game, played with a bat and ball, is something like American baseball. Rugby is a third important team sport. American football was developed from this rough, fast-paced game.

Shoppers stroll through a London shopping arcade (above). Football, known as soccer in America, is very popular with British youth (below).

WORLD

CITIES

London's Surroundings

London is a city of contrasts: the very old versus the very new, busy streets versus quiet parks, world-famous plays in fancy theaters versus sidewalk actors performing in town. Contrast is even seen in the diversity of people that make up London's population. The city's contrast is due, in part, to the fact that London is really a collection of scattered ancient villages. These villages were joined together as the city grew. Many of these areas have retained some of their distinctive village qualities, even though they are now part of Greater London.

The River Thames outlines the city to the south and west. Remember, the oldest section of London, the City, was established right on the bank of the Thames. Through time, the City's government has remained distinct from the rest of London's government. In London, each borough has its own government. This government consists of a council over which a mayor presides. The City, although small, is considered to be equal to the boroughs and retains its own government. This situation was not changed by the creation of the London County Council in 1889 or by the formation of Greater London Council in 1964. Today, the City is the great financial section of London.

Other sections of the city are called Westminster and the West End; stylish Mayfair, Kensington, and Knightsbridge. The central London sections are Soho and Covent Garden. Artists and writers add special qualities and flavor to the sections of Bloomsbury and Chelsea. The section south of the River Thames is called Southwark. London also has the large open spaces of Hyde Park and Regent Park.

Exploring Outer London

Outer London offers some wonderful places to explore. The railways and the underground routes have made the outskirts easy to reach from central London. For some of the areas outside London, it is fun to take a boat along the Thames.

North of the city lies the little village of Hampstead. This village was built on the side of a hill, at the foot of which are the Hampstead Ponds. Hampstead is just 4 miles (6 km) from the center of London. It has been a favorite recreation spot and has always attracted artists, writers, musicians, and scientists. The poet John Keats used to live there, and you can visit his home. For many years, this was a rural area with just a few homes and farms. When springs were discovered, Hampstead became a fashionable spa.

At Tower Pier, near the Tower of London, you can board a boat that will take you downriver, or east, to Greenwich. Once you have docked at Greenwich, on the other side of the river,

The Cutty Sark *was the fastest clipper ship used in the China tea trade.*

there are many things to see. At the Pier is the magnificent ship called the *Cutty Sark*. This clipper was launched in 1869 and used for the China tea trade. It is known especially for its speed.

On shore, you can visit the Tudor Palace, a favorite of the Tudor family and the birthplace of Henry VIII. The Queen's House, a beautiful white palace designed by the architect Inigo Jones, is not too far from there. There is also the Royal Hospital, which was designed by Christopher Wren, and the Royal Naval College. Another important building, also designed by Wren, is the Royal Observatory. Here you can stand with one foot in the Western Hemisphere and one foot in the Eastern Hemisphere. The Prime

Meridian—the imaginary line separating the two hemispheres—passes through the observatory's courtyard.

If you go southwest from central London, you will be able to explore Wimbledon, with its parks and open spaces. This is the home of the world-famous tennis tournament that takes place every summer.

A bit farther southwest, you will come to Hampton Court. The Hampton Court Palace was built for a man named Cardinal Wolsey, but he gave it to Henry VIII as a gift. Henry VIII used this as a place to come to hunt.

During the seventeenth century, Christopher Wren renovated Hampton Court. Today it represents the best of British architecture. When you visit, you can walk through its beautiful state rooms and royal living quarters. Outside are beautiful gardens that form a maze. On one of the towers is a clock that shows twenty-four, not just twelve, hours on its face.

Windsor Castle

Windsor Castle is a little farther outside London. Even so, many people feel that you can't visit London without a trip to Windsor Castle. It is an especially beautiful castle. Although it has been remodeled several times, it still retains the flavor of the eleventh century when it was built. Even a wall

built by the Normans is still standing. Since the time of Henry VIII, the monarchs of Britain have lived here sometime during the year. Queen Elizabeth and her family now live here a few months of the year.

When the royal family is not here,

©Pete Fedynich, Jr./JlG

visitors can walk through their living quarters and St. George's Chapel. Throughout the rooms and hallways, the walls display wonderful works of art by famous painters such as Gainsborough, Hogarth, and Rembrandt. As you can see, whether you are in

Windsor Castle, a royal residence, lies in a parklike setting of lawns and formal gardens.

London or its surrounding towns and villages, you are never far from something that gives you an immense sense of history.

London in the World

London is a world city by virtue of its history. London has survived for more than two thousand years with several beginnings. It was a center for trading ventures that covered the globe. It was the seat of the vast British Empire. What happened in London directly influenced more than one-fifth of the world population at the height of the empire.

London—Still a Political and Economic Center

Although London is not as powerful as it once was, it is still the hub of all the economic and political activity of Great Britain. For example, it is the seat of the Commonwealth of Nations. The Commonwealth is an organiza-tion of countries and other political units once ruled by Britain. The organization includes forty-nine now-independent nations. The European Community (EC) is another important economic organization of which Great Britain is a member. The country joined in 1973. The EC, also known as the European Common Market, over-sees and coordinates the trade of member countries.

London is also the center of much of the world's banking and insurance business. The concentration of banks in the City section of London is higher than anywhere else in the world. It also has the world's largest insurance group—the famous Lloyd's of Lon-don. The Royal Exchange, much like the New York Stock Exchange, influences financial decisions all over the world.

Britain also belongs to important world organizations. One of these is the United Nations (UN). The UN is made up of 159 countries from around the world. It was formed to keep peace and security in the world. Britain also belongs to the North Atlantic Treaty Organization (NATO). NATO, begun in 1950, is a union of sixteen nations. Its purpose is to protect its members against a military attack by eastern European countries or the Soviet Union.

A Center for Tourism

As an important world city, London is an international tourist center. With its unmatched historical attractions such as palaces, churches, theaters, museums, and galleries, tourism will continue to be a sizable industry for London. The city's two airports, Heathrow and Gatwick, handle more international traffic than any other city's airports in the world. Heathrow is located west of the city; Gatwick lies to the south.

A City of Ethnic Groups

The mixture of people in London also makes it a world city. It is home for many ethnic groups, some who came to London from Britain's former

New immigrants have made today's London a mix of many ethnic groups.

territories. These include blacks from Africa and the Caribbean, Asians from India and Vietnam, and people from Cyprus in the Mediterranean.

The first Chinese came to London on the ships of the East India Company in the eighteenth century. They were working on these ships as seamen. When the ships docked in London, many of the Chinese seamen just stayed.

Jewish people began coming to London from northern Europe as early as 1066. Italians began coming to London in the thirteenth century. Many Polish people began coming at the end of the eighteenth century because of political unrest in their homeland.

As you explore the city you will see evidence of this rich ethnic mix: special ethnic restaurants and shops, certain cultural festivals such as the Chinese New Year celebration in Soho, or

the Afro-Caribbean Carnival in Notting Hill.

Many of the groups settled in particular sections of the city. Many Jewish people settled in the city section of London. The Chinese immigrants gathered in Limehouse and later in Soho, and the blacks settled in Brixton. Polish people and now Arabs have settled in Kensington, while many Australians have settled in Earl's Court. Other groups such as the Italians and the Irish have spread throughout the city.

There are many Protestants and Catholics in London. The Church of

Many of London's newest residents have come from Britain's former colonies. Among them are Asians, such as those from India (above), and blacks from the West Indies (below).

England is Protestant. But as ethnic groups came to London, they brought with them their religious beliefs. Now London has many other religions including Judaism (the religion of Jewish people) and Hinduism and Islam from Asia.

The World of the Arts

London has been home to many famous artists and writers. Because of this, it has contributed much to art and literature. Among London's many creative people, William Shakespeare is the most famous. Shakespeare, a playwright and poet, was born in Stratford-on-Avon. This city, which lies northwest of London, is rich with his history. But he lived much of his life in London. His plays, from tragedies such as *Hamlet* to comedies such as *Much Ado About Nothing,* were written in the late 1500s and early 1600s and are considered classics.

But Shakespeare was not alone. British poets William Wordsworth, Lord Byron, and John Keats also lived in or near London. Their poetry is still enjoyed today. Nineteenth-century London contributed novelist Charles Dickens. Dickens's novels gave a realistic view of eighteenth-century London life. Later, in the twentieth century, the Bloomsbury section of London became a popular spot for writers such as Virginia Woolf and D.H. Lawrence.

Two important artists who lived in London were William Blake and John Constable. Blake was a painter and a poet. Constable, also a painter, was famous for his landscape pieces. London is full of museums and art galleries where the works of London artists and artists from all over the world can be enjoyed.

William Shakespeare was only one of the many famous writers that London has given the world.

The Folger Shakespeare Library

During the Christmas season, London takes on the glow of a storybook kingdom.

London has both a Royal Opera and a Royal Ballet. The Royal Ballet began as an extension of the Royal Opera, and both perform in the Royal Opera House in Covent Garden.

There are five symphony orchestras in London. One of these, the Royal Philharmonic, performs in Royal Festival Hall, which was built for the Festival of Britain in 1951. When the Royal Philharmonic performs, it often plays a piece by the composer Ludwig van Beethoven. Beethoven wrote his Ninth Symphony for the Royal Philharmonic and worked closely with it.

London in the Future

London's future depends on its ability to meet the needs of the modern world. London seems to have stepped into the world of computers and finance in grand style and is prepared to meet the challenges of the future. Also, as you have seen, London has an immense history of change and starting over. With the remains of the Roman city Londinium, the ancient Tower of London, the architecture of Wren and Jones, the writings of Shakespeare and Dickens, London carries its past into the future.

London: Historical Events

A.D.
43 The Romans enter Britain to conquer and rule it. They set up a military base in Lyndin, which they later called Londinium.

Early 200s The Romans build a wall around the city.

410 The Romans leave Britain to return home where they are needed in battle.

1066 William the Conqueror, of Normandy, invades Britain.

1067 The White Tower is built for William the Conqueror.

1348 The plague, called the Black Death, strikes Europe. It kills one-fourth of the population.

1509 Henry VIII becomes king of England.

1558 Queen Elizabeth I becomes queen of England. She was the daughter of Henry VIII and his second wife, Anne Boleyn.

1665 The Great Plague kills one-third of London's population.

1666 The Great Fire destroys most of London.

1680 A famous insurance company, Lloyd's, begins business.

1837 Queen Victoria begins her reign. Her sixty-three-year rule was the longest in British history. This period is called the Victorian Age.

1846 London's first railroad station, Euston Station, opens.

1859 Big Ben begins operation. It was installed when Sir Benjamin Hall, who was a large man, was commissioner of works. He was called Big Ben, and the clock was named after him.

1888 The County of London is formed.

1894 The Tower Bridge is built across the River Thames.

1914 World War I begins. Air raids strike London.

1939 Britain enters World War II. London has a great deal of damage from air attacks between the years 1939 and 1945.

1940 Sir Winston Churchill becomes prime minister of Britain.

1953 Elizabeth II is crowned queen of Britain in a colorful ceremony.

1965 Greater London is formed.

1973 Britain becomes a member of the Common Market.

1979 Margaret Thatcher becomes prime minister of Britain.

Central London

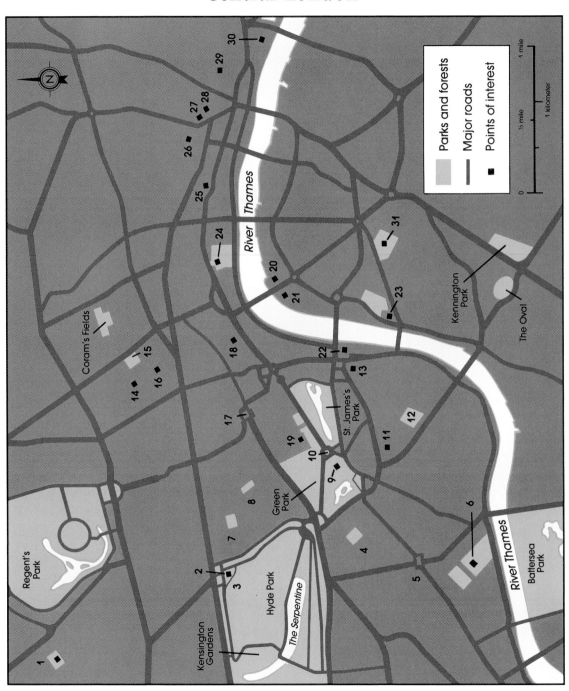

Parks and forests

Major roads

Points of interest

Regent's Park

Coram's Fields

River Thames

Kennington Park

The Oval

St James's Park

Green Park

Hyde Park

The Serpentine

Kensington Gardens

Battersea Park

River Thames

½ mile · 1 mile

1 kilometer

Map Key

London Almanac

Location: Latitude—51.3° north. Longitude—1° west.

Climate: Temperate—overcast over half of the year. Average January temperature—41°F (5°C). Average July temperature—62°F (17°C). Average annual precipitation—24 inches (61 cm).

Land Area: 610 sq. miles (1,580 sq. km).

Population: 6,851,400 people (1981 census). World ranking—8. Population density—11,231 persons/sq. mile.

Major Airports: Heathrow Airport—34,742,100 passengers a year. Gatwick Airport—19,372,600 passengers a year.

Colleges/Universities: 40 colleges, universities, and other institutions of higher learning, including University of London. Some of its schools include Hethrop College, Birkbeck College, Queen Mary College, King's College, and Westfield College.

Medical Facilities: Hospitals—100. Hospital beds—53,000. Doctors—30,000. Nurses—56,000.

Media: Newspapers—main newspapers are *The London Times, The Guardian, The Daily Telegraph, The Sun,* and *The Daily Mirror.* Radio—1 commercial station run by Independent Broadcasting Association (IBA). Television—2 stations: British Broadcasting Company and Independent Broadcasting Association.

Major Buildings: Shell Centre—26 stories, approximately 290 feet (88 m). National Westminster Bank—54 stories, approximately 600 feet (183 m). Post Office Tower—619 feet (189 m).

Port: Port of London—44,046 tons/year.

Transportation: 100 miles (161 km) of underground rail (subway).

Bridges: Battersea Bridge, Blackfriars Bridge, London Bridge, Westminster Bridge—all spanning the River Thames.

Interesting Fact: London's subway system is the largest in the world.

Index